CRYSTAL HEALING MEDITATION

DISCOVER THE SECRET HEALING POWER OF GEMSTONES & CRYSTALS USING GUIDED MEDITATION

ADESH SILVA

© **Copyright 2020 - All rights reserved.**

The content contained within this book may not be reproduced, duplicated or transmitted without direct written permission from the author or the publisher.

Under no circumstances will any blame or legal responsibility be held against the publisher, or author, for any damages, reparation, or monetary loss due to the information contained within this book, either directly or indirectly.

Legal Notice:

This book is copyright protected. It is only for personal use. You cannot amend, distribute, sell, use, quote or paraphrase any part, or the content within this book, without the consent of the author or publisher.

Disclaimer Notice:

Please note the information contained within this document is for educational and entertainment purposes only. All effort has been executed to present accurate, up to date, reliable, complete information. No warranties of any kind are declared or implied. Readers acknowledge that the author is not engaged in the rendering of legal, financial, medical or professional advice. The content within this book has been derived from various sources. Please consult a licensed professional before attempting any techniques outlined in this book.

By reading this document, the reader agrees that under no circumstances is the author responsible for any losses, direct or indirect, that are incurred as a result of the use of the information contained within this document, including, but not limited to, errors, omissions, or inaccuracies.

CONTENTS

Introduction — 5

1. THE HISTORY OF HEALING CRYSTALS — 11
   - How They Form — 13
   - What They're Used For — 16
   - Common Beliefs — 18

2. EFFECTS OF CRYSTALS ON YOURSELF — 21
   - Why You Might Want to Use Them — 23
   - The Symptoms of Emotional Damage — 25
   - Healing the Emotional Pain — 27

3. PICKING YOUR CRYSTAL & MAKING YOUR GRID — 29
   - Types of Healing Crystals — 31
   - How to Pick the Right Ones — 36
   - Creating Your Grid — 39

4. MEDITATION WITH CRYSTALS — 43
   - Using Crystals for Meditation — 45
   - Creating Your Meditation Space — 46
   - Common Mistakes to Avoid — 48

5. GUIDED MEDITATION WITH CRYSTALS — 51
   - The Meditation — 54

6. HEALING MEDITATION WITH CRYSTALS — 64
   - The Meditation — 67

7. RELAXING MEDITATION WITH CRYSTALS	87
The Meditation	91
Conclusion	99
References	103

INTRODUCTION

When was the last time you felt truly relaxed? Most of us seek pleasure where we can from life but are unable to elicit a steady level of consistent relaxation.

Meditation is one of the best natural forms of healing for mental and even physical health. For some, this mindfulness practice can be challenging at first. Freeing yourself from those dark thoughts can be a challenge, and that process might be uncomfortable for some. However, it's crucial to train your brain to self-mediate to prevent anxiety from taking over.

One method to help enhance meditational practices is through the use of crystals. Adding crystals to your daily meditation can take your relaxation to the next level. Alter-

INTRODUCTION

nately, they can provide a foundation and focal point for those who are just beginning to meditate.

Over 4,000 types of crystals and gemstones have been discovered. The vastness of these rocks is not limited to what we already know either. In fact, many scientists have concluded that the Earth's core is surrounded by a solid crystal—one that could be as thick as 1,500 miles (Broad, 1995).

Though there are countless crystals in existence, I am only going to focus on a few that are used specifically for healing.

What does healing mean to you? For some, it looks like a scab, a scar, or recovering from illness. But healing isn't always physical. Healing the mind is just as important as restoring the body.

Meditating using crystals can be beneficial to your life in many ways. Anxiety and fear can keep us trapped in the same place for too long. We miss out on opportunities, run away from issues, and crumble under the smallest ounce of pressure when we don't give our mentality much effort.

As a father of two, a meditation aficionado, and a spiritual enthusiast, it's important for me to share my knowledge with others so they can find the same peaceful healing that has helped me navigate positively throughout life.

Harnessing the healing energy of crystals is not easy the first time you try, but it does get simpler the more you practice. To take some of the work out of this beginner's process, I have created a simple guide to understanding crystals. The last three chapters also involve long-form meditation to help you unlock your spirituality and get closer to being the person you really are deep inside.

Self-growth is what keeps us progressing throughout life. How can anyone flourish if they are staying hidden in a shell? How can you enhance your life by doing the same thing all the time? Valuable change requires effort. That work is hard to do when we can't focus or concentrate. Worse, some people might not even be spiritually aware enough to realize their life requires change.

Healing crystals will help you find your spiritual strength. It is a process you must experience on your own. It is one that will require deep thought that becomes easier to navigate with the use of meditation.

There is energy all around us. The music you listen to can change your mood. Something you smell might trigger a memory. The things you see can make you laugh or cry. Someone else's bad mood might erase your good one (or vice versa). A bright, cheery smile might turn your grumpiness around. These are all experiences in which energy transfers

INTRODUCTION

from one point to another. Where it came from doesn't always matter, but instead it's what you do with that energy that will make the greatest difference.

The circle of energy we have is affected by a variety of factors. Picking and choosing what you bring into that circle will help you better control the energy you feel and elicit.

Crystals are rocks grown naturally from the earth. Just like we have been uniquely shaped and transformed throughout our lives, crystals have gone through a similar, unique process.

Think of other things from the earth that can impact us. The food we eat, the water we drink, and the people we interact with all come from this same planet on which we all exist. These things can be healing, so who is to say that a rock grown and shaped by the earth cannot do the same?

They can help more with mental healing. Our minds are so vast and powerful that it's easy to lose control of them. Scary thoughts can become exacerbated by even worse fears piling on top. Frantic rumination can lead to impulsive decisions that worsen the negative emotions we already have.

Our minds have their own healing powers. Harnessing that healing power isn't as natural for some as it is for others. In order to gain that ability, a bit of focus is required. This is where meditation comes into play. Meditation requires us to step away from our routines to focus on clearing our mind. All day thoughts can pile up so meditation is the cleansing process that washes those away. It's a form of concentration that makes it easier to focus on our goals and get rid of the cluttered ideas that prevent them from reaching those milestones.

When meditating, you must find a quiet space to focus on nothing but your breathing. Emptying your mind can be a challenge but a crystal can make that process much stronger. It provides additional energy to assist you with the mental work you're putting in as you go about your life.

The collision of energy will help you center yourself, so you can finally focus on healing to free your mind from consistent negativity. Think about how music can help you work out easier. It pumps you up and gives you a focal point so the burn in your legs isn't so bad. Having a white noise machine on when you go to sleep might make it easier to drown out any minor noises that keep your mind wandering all night.

Whatever energy you hope to gain is what will guide you to pick a crystal. Filling your motives will enable you to strengthen your self-healing abilities. Crystals are assistants, not total cures. They accessorize your healing process but are not the foundation. You can't just hold a crystal and

INTRODUCTION

make a wish. It's not a genie in a bottle or a magical wand. A crystal is a source for you to push off from, not unlike the bottom of a swimming pond. It is the railing you hold onto as you climb the stairs. Crystals are powerful, but only when you help to harness that power internally rather than depending on external circumstances.

1

THE HISTORY OF HEALING CRYSTALS

The use of natural elements for healing dates back as far as recorded history. We can't say for certain when it started, but we do know that stones and crystals and their long history are intertwined with alternative medicine.

Ancient Egyptians used stones and crystals in jewelry, but believed in their magical properties as well. They would often use stones to help with sleep and warding off nightmares. Ancient Greeks used crystals for healing—and gave many of them the names we still use today.

In most cultures you will be able to find at least some evidence that crystals have been used for healing. Whether they were worn as jewelry, pulverized for makeup, or valued simply as a possession, crystals have played important roles in human history.

Perhaps the best reference for how far back crystal use goes comes from Sungir, Russia. A grave was uncovered that was determined to date back more than 60,000 years. In the grave, beads were found that had been made from shells and shark teeth. Amulet use provides a reference for how certain cultures used certain tools for spiritual and healing purposes.

The fact that amulets, crystals, stones, talisman, and other spiritual tools are often found on bodies, in graves, and in tombs shows us they were very important to these people at the time.

Though the Christian Church banned amulets in 355 AD, stones and crystals continued to play a crucial role in various spiritual practices.

It wasn't until as recently as the 1980s that a new resurgence of crystal use for healing began to grow. Today, more and more individuals have turned to alternative medicine in our modern times. Whether it's a decorative store with items on a shelf or a necklace adorned with them, crystals are everywhere.

Those seeking alternative medicinal practices can find value from crystal use. On one hand, we are more aware than ever of our mental health. At the same time, not everybody wants to take medicine, nor do we have true "cures" for mental health problems. For this reason, spiritual practices using outside resources like crystals have become more popular. It's low stakes, there are no side effects to it, and you can train yourself to heal your mental ailments on your own.

HOW THEY FORM

In the simplest terms, crystals can be defined as hardened liquids.

They form naturally through a cooling process as they harden. Various molecules arrange into specific patterns. These repeated designs form beautiful, sparkling, colorful, bright crystals. Naturally, crystals are rugged; they have sharp edges. They have cracks and crevices.

There are different ways that crystals can be shaped and formed. Raw crystals are thought by some to be the most powerful. They are untouched by man and can be viewed in their natural state. Some believe they are purer than others and will provide a more substantial power to the person using them. They might be easier to feel a connection to because they are so natural.

However, a crystal is still a crystal. At the end of the day, it is up to you to decide if you would like to seek only natural crystals or if you are more interested in tumbled and cut versions.

Tumbled crystals are smooth like rocks. They look like stones. Even though they share the same pattern as other crystals. They have been created specifically for this design. They often come very small and can be held in your hand. You can keep them in your pocket and touch them as needed. You can place them in your clothing. Some people will even wear tumbled stones in their bras because it's close to their heart.

Cut crystals often look like specific shapes. You might have a double-edged pointed crystal or perhaps a geometric shape. Cut crystals are not man-made. They are taken from nature and shaped by man, this doesn't mean that they're any less beautiful than others. Pointed crystals can help you when directional energy is needed. If you're performing a meditation to help bring health and peace to your family, you might point it outward toward others. If you're simply doing an internal healing, you might keep your crystals directed toward yourself.

Geodes and other partial crystals might be smoothed down on one side but still have some natural elements at the others. Some crystals are heat treated, which helps bring out their patterns and vibrancy. There is no correct standard for how to collect crystals. If you would like, you can be somebody who only has natural crystals. You might only want small tumbled crystals, so they're easier to carry around.

A good crystal collection is usually rather eclectic. Pick crystals that you are drawn to whether they simply look beautiful or you're interested in the natural properties they have. Picking a gemstone that calls your name will be the most effective when choosing crystals. It's simply important that you determine whether they are authentic. An authentic tumbled crystal is more powerful than a man-made crystal that was engineered to look real. A natural crystal is a crystal, regardless of whether it was picked up straight from the ground or has been shaped and smoothed and passed around from person to person for years. A man-made crystal is still a crystal, but it's the energy that will differ. A natural crystal gets its energy from the long formation process it went through. This could mean years of energy absorption from its surroundings. A man-made crystal can still absorb energy, but since they can sometimes be mass-produced, there might not be any healing powers. Instead they can serve as decorative items, which can be just as powerful as genuine healing crystals for some.

To summarize, find what makes you comfortable and what you are drawn to in order to gain the most from these powerful stones.

WHAT THEY'RE USED FOR

Each crystal has its own purpose. Some crystals are better for healing interpersonal issues. Others might be used for helping you improve your love life. Crystals can be used specifically for healing or just general emotional maintenance. In general, crystals are used for whatever you want to use them for. Crystal use can be very broad and it might overwhelm you at first. That's why it's important to look at specific crystals, figure out what you want or what you feel drawn to, and then do your research accordingly.

In this book I'm going to focus specifically on healing crystals, including several of my personal favorites.

Crystals are used as a grounding tool to help keep you more connected to a certain issue you might have. If you're sitting there feeling anxious, stressed, and overwhelmed, it's hard to know where to start. This process of healing is one that is done mentally.

There is no pill that will take all of your mental pain away. You can take certain medications that will assist in the mental healing you're undergoing, but nothing is going to be an instant cure-all. If you have a cut, a scrape, or a bruise on your body, you don't just put a Band-Aid on it and it instantly goes away. It's going to need a few days. It might even get worse at one point as it cleanses and heals itself.

Eventually, there might be a scar after the healing process is done. As you go through that process, you might use different creams or ointments. You might have to take a pain reliever. You might even have to go to the hospital. You put a Band-Aid on it and you still have to clean it with alcohol and soap on a daily basis.

The mental process is similar. Nothing is going to be an instant fix, but crystals are like the ointment or the Band-Aid or the pain reliever that will help assist you in this healing process to make it easier.

Different crystals hold different energies. That is why it's important to know what it is that you want to heal. If you have the cut on your knee, you don't put ointment on your entire body. You start first by putting ointment on where the specific cut might be. Eventually that cut could get infected and affect the rest of your body. That is when you would start to do more general healing. But first we must look at the source of the sickness. From there you can begin to seek out the crystals that can aid you in that process.

If you have sunburn, you don't put an anti-itch ointment for bug bites on that patch of skin; you would use aloe Vera to help alleviate that pain.

In chapter three, I'm going to go over specific types of crystals. But first I just wanted to cover basically what crystals are used for. They can be held in your hand as a focus object. You can wear them on jewelry as protection. You can place them around your home for decoration.

They're not ground up or mixed with ointment. They're not consumed or eaten. They exist as grounding objects that stay with you. They are unique in the ability to help you heal externally while working through those internal processes.

COMMON BELIEFS

As I mentioned in the beginning of this chapter, crystals have been an important part of many cultures. Like herbs, clay, and even water, crystals provide an organic healing power that goes beyond culture and instead relates to humanity as a whole. We are not the only species to use outside objects for healing. On the simplest level, think of how a tiger uses a tree to scratch its back or a deer licks a salty rock for the minerals they provide. Some species will use more complex healing methods. Chimpanzees eat certain plants with rough bristles or spiky leaves to help clear their stomach or soothe digestive-related pain. Some elephants have even eaten certain leaves from trees to help induce labor (Shurkin, 2014). Self-healing across different species reminds us that not only do these methods work, but the ability to soothe ones' own ailments is a natural instinct wired into our anatomy.

The most common belief about crystals is that they hold energy.

Crystals vibrate. In fact, everything vibrates. All things that exist on our great planet have a certain level of frequency. Those who practice crystal use believe that these vibrations will affect one another. This is something that isn't seen but rather felt. Have you ever walked into a room after two people had just finished fighting? Maybe your parents quickly stopped talking after you heard them arguing from the other room. You can sense the tension even if not looking at their faces. Have you ever been around someone extremely cheery and positive? You might have felt more relaxed just being in their presence.

When you're holding these crystals, you won't feel it vibrate like you would your phone if you got a text or call. However, the deeper energy beneath these vibrations is what affects our body's energy. Crystals help us find those "good vibes" and focus on them while meditating. The energy of a crystal can be harvested and used to help heal our own energy.

Many people remain skeptical because crystals are dependent on a user's interpretation. It's not like a magic pill that will make you feel better physically without you trying. To see the power of crystals one must make an effort. If you remain skeptical, you will fail to see how the crystals work.

The way crystals can repair your spirit and assist in your healing is powerful, but only if you have an open mind and are willing to put in the work. The connection you have to crystals is one that can only be felt and experienced by you. This deeper understanding isn't taught or given but rather simply felt by the individual crystal user.

Whether crystals will work for you is up to the mentality you have surrounding them. For example, think of your dreams. Not the hopes and desires of the future, but the actual dream imagery you have when you're sleeping. Some people can easily interpret these dreams and make use of them. A dream you're in the passenger's seat of a moving car with no driver might indicate you feel out of control. At the same time, it could just feel like a chaotic nightmare that you forget about. A dream can be a tool to help you grow, or it can just be a crazy memory you have. The dream exists as it is. It is up to you to determine whether or how this will be used in your healing process. The same goes for horoscopes. If you believe in the power of astrology, you will likely be able to pull some interpretation from your daily forecast. If you're skeptical, you might read the horoscope with that critical eye and look for things to validate your skepticism rather than seeking things to convince you of the validity.

The true magic of crystals lies within the power that you choose to give to them.

2

EFFECTS OF CRYSTALS ON YOURSELF

Some healing methods can have side effects. For example, a medication for pain might make you drowsy. A cast for a broken bone can limit mobility. Crystal healing has very few side effects.

Sometimes deep reflection and meditation might take you down a mental path you're not prepared for. Confronting inner thoughts and working through trauma might be scary. It could mean reliving painful memories. Crystals will provide a grounding aspect through this mental processing. Though the intention is to relax and soothe you as you heal, our minds can still surprise us, especially at the beginning. Having a crystal with you builds your resilience against dark thoughts that flood the mind. They boost your energy, increase your focus, and enhance your will power.

Crystals can help provide emotional stability when feelings become overwhelming. You can use the crystals as a manifestation of your energy, transferring negative thoughts and feelings to the crystal element. Then, you can wash the crystals or cleanse them in a salt bath to rid yourself of negative feelings.

Crystals can have physical effects as well. You can wear one in your pocket as you go for a nature walk. They can be protectors in your carry-on bag while flying, or maybe under your mattress or on your nightstand. A crystal on your forehead might alleviate a headache. You can even purchase crystal-infused water bottles to help gain more of the healing benefits that crystals have to offer.

Crystals will be more effective when time is taken to charge them. Like we need food to energize and relaxation to strengthen us also, crystals need time to gain energy as well. Crystal changes are subtle, but they are there; think of the way a Himalayan salt lamp might sweat. The process of charging or "energizing" a crystal is an important part of what will make it more effective during meditation.

Energizing is a relatively straightforward process. You can charge them during a full moon. Wait for a full moon, then place the crystals outside or on a windowsill, where the moon will be able to directly shine on them. Leave them out for the duration of the full moon to notice a deep charge.

You can do the same for the sun with certain crystals, but many, like amethyst or rose quartz, shouldn't be exposed to long durations of sunshine.

A cleansing salt bath will help create a more pristine and balanced direction of energy emitted from the crystals. You can toss them in a bowl with salt for a dry bath, while some crystals can be cleansed in water. Before purchasing, do your research on how to bathe the crystal of choice.

One of the most successful ways of making your crystals more efficient is to meditate with that crystal. This way, you are placing specific energy on that object. You are taking the time out of your day to channel as much energy as possible into this specific source. You then hold this energy and are able to use it as you wish. Having an outlet for our energy is perfect for the healing process. We need to purge ourselves of the negativity and toxicity that has plagued our minds. That makes it important to replenish our spirit with the positive energy that crystals provide.

WHY YOU MIGHT WANT TO USE THEM

There are many things we experience in our lives that can break our spirit. As young babies and children, we are naturally happy and joyous when nurtured. The simple sight of our parents can make us smile and giggle. We think it's funny when something drops or a person makes a silly noise. As we grow older, our curiosity begins to expand, and we see the world as this amazing and mesmerizing place. Simple things continue to provide us with so much excitement.

But sometimes, the older we get, the more that our spirit gets broken.

The excited curiosity that we once had as children slowly fades through age. Some can easily maintain that happy persona, but others struggle under the increasing pressures of adulthood.

Alleviation is sought by the pained heart, and sometimes it can lead to destructive decisions. Alcohol, drugs, food, and other vices cloud judgement and exacerbate the mental anguish. Layer after layer of hurt is piled on until our aching souls can't take it anymore.

Healing is an ongoing process but one that will become more normal with practice. You might choose to use crystals to enhance your abilities to heal from pains of the past.

Anxiety over small things like work can feel like the end of the world. Stressors involving peers, family, and other things can weigh on our hearts. Now it is the time to allow vibrational energies into your plane of living. By embracing the natural elements of crystals, you will be controlling where the energy exists in your life. It will awaken your ability to connect to a deeper feeling. Crystals are a vessel to a different level of vitality. Untapping this pool of deeper meaning will give you the chance to heal old wounds and strengthen your defenses for the future.

THE SYMPTOMS OF EMOTIONAL DAMAGE

Some of the symptoms of emotional damage that you have are very clear and obvious. You might be afraid to fall in love again because you've been hurt so many times in the past. You might be seeking comfort and satisfaction from other people because you've been treated poorly by others. However, there are plenty of symptoms of emotional damage deep beneath the surface that we don't even realize. These pains become so normal to us that we don't try to actively change them because they seem like they are simply a part of who we are.

For example, think of common thought patterns. One is polarized thinking. This is the idea that everything is on an "either-or" scenario. It's a type of black-and-white thought process where you must put everything into a category. If you wake up in the morning and are running late for work, automatically it turns into a bad day. If you have one negative experience with a waitress at a restaurant, you might never want to visit that place again. If somebody gives you a funny look, you might assume they hate you and you never want to talk to them again. We instantly label everything as either good or bad. The thing is, it's really easy to see the bad in even the best of things. Eventually, everything becomes awful, thereby creating a negative mindset where we exist in this world full of terrible things.

While it's true that the word does have some negative aspects, that is not a reason to hate our lives; it's also filled with just as many beautiful things. We can rise above the adversity and still flourish even when bad things happen. An inability to manage emotions can lead to negative self-talk. In a world that sometimes doesn't make sense, we seek meaning to have greater understanding. For those who constantly self-blame, it's hard to not view everything as your fault. You might belittle yourself to the point that you are your own greatest bully.

Sometimes in an attempt to feel better, we might also form a perspective of perfectionism. You likely hold yourself above others in that you see their faults as acceptable while yours are a reason to punish yourself. You might be competitive, contradictive, and combative.

This inner struggle leads us to assume the worst. Rather than fully preparing for the future, it's easy to become panicked and afraid that only the worst-case scenario is possible. These emotional mood swings and extreme sensitivities can be overwhelming.

As we begin to heal emotional damage, these feelings can become more manageable, leading to a higher quality of life.

HEALING THE EMOTIONAL PAIN

There are a few rules to healing I believe are the most important when using meditation and crystals. Of course, these aren't strict rules that offer punishment if they are broken, but instead serve as guidelines we can follow as we heal.

The first rule is: Be willing to put in the work. This isn't a process that someone else can do for you. Healing comes from within, and though external sources are used to enhance the outcome, the majority of your growth is still found within. To heal is to plant a seed that you are committed to growing. It requires attention and care every day. Even if you don't take any active steps to water or prune it, simply admiring the beauty of the growth will help it energize and flourish. Nourish your soul and spirit by working out the tough parts of your mentality. Confront negative thoughts and take the opportunity to elicit peace.

Second: Get comfortable with being uncomfortable. You might have to admit—more than once—that you were wrong. You might realize a hard lesson from deep reflection. You might get reminded of something you wanted to forget.

Though challenging, it is this kind of discomfort that will garner you the most growth. Meditation carries outside of the practice in that way. But it is the relaxing ritual you do which will soothe any pain throughout the healing process.

Pay attention to the inner voice you have. You know the one. It's buried deep down; sometimes it doesn't exist, and in other moments it flares up and screams at you.

Stay fluid with your healing. Don't get stuck in one place. Healing is like climbing a set of stairs. You want to keep climbing. The further up you go, the harder it will be for you to want to go back down. Keep pushing on and you'll realize that greatness has been waiting for you all along. Always seek growth and change. If it feels like you're plateauing, it's time to try something new.

Take it day by day. You cannot predict your own emotions. As much as you might make effort in your emotional healing, there will always be days where you don't feel 100%. The most important thing to do is keep moving. Since you will have crystals long after you're done with a meditation session, they will act as placeholders for this emotional healing. They will always be reminders that you must continue growing and prospering.

3

PICKING YOUR CRYSTAL & MAKING YOUR GRID

The healing process is unique. Only you know the experiences that you've lived through, so only you will know the tools it takes to heal. Our bodies give us signals of what's wrong; becoming more aware means you'll be able to better decipher those messages.

Where is your stress being held? Stress is a natural response to things that seem overwhelming, chaotic, or hard to understand. We feel stress emotionally but it can also manifest in our bodies. Tense jaws, achy shoulders, and sore muscles all over could indicate that you're not properly managing stressful situations.

What are you carrying? Guilt? Responsibility? Pressure? These things can be so challenging to manage that they weigh on our shoulders like a ton of bricks. Look at what your body is trying to protect to begin to awaken your spirit to the secrets hidden inside. If you feel as though finances are pressing down on you, it could make your shoulders feel tense. You're carrying the burden of providing for you and your family, so it's easy to let the pressure build up. If you're not living truthfully or speaking your mind, maybe it'll cause a tense jaw as you keep your lips tight and teeth clenched. What our bodies tell us is not always black and white, but it's crucial we don't overlook hidden secrets.

How many times have you lost an entire day because of an angry mood when you first woke up? Guilt, anger, regret, frustration, and anxiety are all hard to manage. Though sometimes it feels easier to just be negative, it's taking away more from us than we might think.

Stress is supposed to be an important tool for survival. What was once a savior from predators and other natural threats has now become a point of frustration and fixation. Rather than helping us to survive, stress is literally killing some. Heart disease is the leading cause of death in the U.S. alone, taking over half a million lives every year. While the food we eat plays a huge role in that high number, stress has many indirect, and direct, relations to these deaths as well. We've all turned to food as a comfort during a stressful period in life at some point. Excessive overeating and binge-eating disorders can exacerbate the negative effects stress is already taking on your hormones and digestive system. Many also turn to smoking and excessive drinking as a relief from life's greatest pains. The heart is a mighty organ, but bombarding it with stress, unhealthy food, and unhealthy coping mechanisms will eventually take its toll.

Crystals aren't the only healing tools to use. Remember hobbies and fun activities can also replenish our spirits. Keep crystals with you when you're doing things you enjoy as this could also help charge their energies. For example, if you're hanging out and having a game night with friends, why not light a candle and set a crystal out at the same time? The laughter and happy conversations could fuel this energy so when you need a pick-me-up during a bad mood, the crystal could help.

Everyone should strive to exercise and maintain a healthy diet as well. Keep a crystal with you when you are doing a challenging exercise, as it could boost your mood and provide protection against pain. The self-doubt you have when on a treadmill can be alleviated by a healing crystal. They offer support for things beyond just meditation!

TYPES OF HEALING CRYSTALS

Pick crystals that you are drawn to. Seek methods of incorporating these into your meditation routines. When your collection is large enough, you will be able to make a crystal chart that will provide even more energy for your ritual practices. For now, I want to start with ten very basic healing crystals. I want to keep it limited so as to not overwhelm you. During the three meditations of the book, you will only need crystals that you already have or ones that you plan to purchase. I wanted to keep it general so beginners would not feel too pressured. Regardless of what you decide to purchase, I have provided a list of my favourites. These are all great for beginners and offer a starting point for those who want to eventually grow their collections. They are relatively inexpensive and easy to find. The price of a crystal does not mean it is any more or less powerful. Some crystals are only more valuable because they are harder to get, but you can still find strength in the inexpensive small ones.

Clear quartz is the most basic crystal you will want to incorporate in your collection. If you have zero crystals, this is a good first purchase. It is very general and provides fundamental healing properties. This crystal will help unlock certain parts of your mind and is a great stone for beginners. It will absorb whatever intention you might want to give it while also supporting other crystals. It will enhance any healing meditation, chart, or other spiritual practice. Clear quartz can be carried for protection. Some will place it in their plants to help them grow or underneath their pillows to absorb dreams.

Amethyst is a great second addition. This beautiful purple stone is very popular and is likely to be found in certain department or "big box" stores. (Be cautious, however, because they might be fake!) Amethyst is important for emotional healing. This precious gemstone also can be used to enhance a person's love life. Whether you are looking to improve your love life or the relationship you have with yourself, amethyst offers emotional pain relief while soothing the aches of life. This tranquil crystal helps to reduce some of the stress you might feel. This crystal helps bring you closer to your spirituality, and some have even felt personally called to amethyst. This calling can present itself in many different ways. Some are naturally more drawn to it while others might even hear a voice that leads them to a specific location where the amethyst can be found. All crystals can provide a calling; it's about the user's experience and what they feel personally connected to.

Selenite is known as a basic protector. It offers luck as well, making it a great assistant in the healing process. Selenite also has a very open energy which makes it great for cleansing. It will absorb negativity around you while serving as a blank slate if you'd like to charge it with a certain power. This peaceful crystal will soothe any fear you have as you go through the healing process. It will be especially helpful for recovery related to trauma, because it can also impart clarity.

Obsidian is one of the most indestructible materials on the planet. For that reason, it's a very good tool for protection. Those who might fear getting hurt again will often get held back, so knowing that you have a protector on your side like obsidian can increase confidence and improve overall strength. Those who have been taken advantage of and repeatedly hurt by others can find strength and protection from obsidian. It's also a magnet that will be useful in pulling out dark spiritual feelings.

Rose quartz is another beautiful and essential stone for your healing. The vibrations of this stone can have healing powers for your heart. Rose quartz can lead you beyond the superficial aspects of love while also forgiving past mistakes. Healing this part of yourself enables personal growth and new opportunities.

Citrine offers positivity through its beauty. This form of encouragement and motivation is absolutely essential in the healing process. Citrine has a friendly energy that becomes contagious. This warm, reassuring gemstone adds an element of hope to your charts. It will unlock your solar plexus chakra, which exists in your chest. This adds a boost of self-esteem to serve as a reminder that you are capable of anything.

Moonstone acts as a stabilizer for your emotions. Remaining grounded enables you to truly unlock deeper inspiration. Growing your intuition can lead to greater success. This stone is a must for those looking to heal their professional or creative lives. Just as the moon rises every night, the moonstone constantly provides new beginnings.

Agate comes in many colors. It's similar to crystal quartz in that it can have a general energy to be manipulated by outside sources. You can pick a specific agate to help guide you with your intention. For example, blue agate can be good for washing away trauma so you can start anew after healing. Dendritic agate will help provide earthly powers through fate and abundance. If you have been suffering or lost, moss agate could also connect you back to the earth. This reminds you of your own existence, forcing an awareness which could lead to enlightenment.

Lapis lazuli is a healing staple, as it's used specifically for healing from trauma. This royal blue crystal provides guidance as one unravels their trauma. Finding meaning, understanding, and purpose in the experiences we've lived through promotes a deeper connection to these challenging memories.

Tourmaline is a grounding stone which means it can be very beneficial for meditation. It also helps unlock a more spiritual energy in the user. This mystical crystal has healing powers that will be felt vibrationally during rituals and meditative practices.

In some of the meditations I might mention other stones, like those used for your chakra. Just because you might not have a specific stone does not mean you can't still gain power from these practices. All you truly need for these meditations is one simple stone that you can use to focus and center on throughout the meditations.

HOW TO PICK THE RIGHT ONES

You have to pick crystals based on your healing journey. Picking crystals specific to your intention allows you to have a deeper connection. It makes your goals more feasible, especially in the process of healing.

Of course, the main goal for many is to soothe their deepest pains and grow their inner strength. This is only done when you're able to recognize the parts of your life that need healing in this moment. What aspects do you feel are missing pieces? Where would you like to find more life, integrity, and meaning? The healing process isn't just so we can feel better after. It's important that throughout our journeys we look for ways to ensure we never have to live through these kinds of things again. If we do experience them, we need the tools, like crystals, to help protect us from that familiar pain.

Crystals can literally be placed on parts of your body that might need healing. The vibrations they give off will affect the vibrations of your body. The closer you can get these two to each other, the more magnetism will be present. This strong bond will enable you to fight off the pain and hurt and begin to replenish yourself. The planes of energy you have are not so easily measured, so choosing the right crystals will be determined by how they make you feel and the connection you share with them.

Do you want the crystal to take something away or give something to you? Like a sponge, crystals can be used to sop up all the negative feelings you wish to purge from your soul. If you're in the beginning of your healing process, it's likely there are a lot of built-up tensions and negative emotions you are desperate to get rid of. If you've just come out of a terrible relationship, bad living situation, or another traumatic event, it's in your best interest to pick specific crystals to help absorb those negative energies.

For example, Jasper is a beginner-friendly crystal that will help take on some of those feelings. If you are wanting to get more benefits from the crystal, you might choose a more intense gemstone like Bloodstone. This is thought to literally cleanse your body, giving you an extra boost when recovering.

Determine your intention. This is a more general goal, like creating positive change in the world or building abundance. This intention will give you a focal point throughout your meditations making it easier to know where to shift your thoughts. Even if you don't have a clear intention, that exact issue could lead to your motive. You might want to seek self-discovery and get to know yourself better. Your intention could be to find the very things that you actually desire after living a life that belonged to someone else.

What do you need? Why are you unable to provide these things for yourself? A crystal can only do so much for you; you have to put in more work than any gemstone. If you are seeking too much from the crystals, that could only grow your frustrations. Ensure your intention isn't too specific or grand, or else you'll just be setting yourself up for failure.

How can you tell what it is that you need? Are you discovering these intentions on your own, or are you depending on someone else's words to determine what your needs are? It's not always easy to even know what we want, let alone how to get it.

What are you hoping to gain from this meditation? What are you going to give in order to get that? The efforts you might have to put in could be sacrificial. You might have to put in more time. Maybe you redirect away from a goal in favor of another goal that's more realistic for the time being. You might have to postpone a life event, especially if it means reevaluating if it's what you want. While this process doesn't have to be tortuous, it's not always easy either. The more we brush aside our mental health, the more uncomfortable it might get.

CREATING YOUR GRID

Additional objects can be placed in or around your crystal grid to enhance the powers. If you want to repair a relationship during a meditation, you might have a picture of the person you're struggling with. If you want to increase your abundance, you might include a piece of jewelry or other monetary offering. Perhaps you're going to open yourself up even more. You can use incense or essential oils in an air diffuser to tap deeper into your senses. A background, natural noise like water or wind could be an additional way to soothe you.

The crystals that you pick will mix and mingle with these aspects. Let yourself truly mix and mingle with your crystal arrangement. You will be able to feel on your own if something fits or if you need to make some adjustments.

A grid is the connection among your crystals. It creates a stable layout that binds the energies in a unifying manner. Imagine a shape that is seen in the stars. It's not that you can see the lines, but when you step back and let your eyes fill in the spaces between these stars, images form.

Symmetry also helps to create a balance. For example, create a pentagon or hexagon shape with your crystals. You will see the straight lines that can connect each one.

Once you have chosen the right intention, it's now time to move on to the creation of your grid. This should be a hope, a dream, or a great desire that you want to incorporate into your life. Begin by writing this intention down on a piece of paper. You can use a natural element like charcoal to write the message down. If you can't put it into words, you can also use images or sketches to help give a visualization to the things that you are intending to get from these meditations. Write this down on a piece of paper and fold it at least twice.

Use cleansed crystals as you prepare for a new meditation. You can charge them and reuse them for an additional power, but for first-time use they should always be cleansed. Remember that not all crystals can be washed in water or with salt, so be cautious before proceeding with your bathing ritual. Cleansing them ensures you are starting with a clean slate. It's hard to know what kinds of energies these crystals absorbed before they made their way into your hands.

Use a clear crystal quartz for the center of your grid. This is the most basic stone and a powerful spiritual one that will act as a connection between the rest of the grid. Underneath the crystal should be the folded paper with your intention. By placing this clear quartz on top of the grid, you are prepping it to absorb the message you're desiring.

Around this stack should be the remainder of your crystals. You can spread it out as far as you would like, but it should still be contained within a space small enough for you to sit in front of. As you practice with grid creation, you can begin expanding them and even taking them outdoors. Some will use crystals to create a protective boundary around their home.

Use the crystal quartz to touch each crystal in the grid. Work your way from the outermost layer and slowly connect them together as you move in. Take your time with this step and feel as the energies combine. Tapping each crystal is your way to activate them. Eventually they will begin vibrating together, allowing for your intention to become even more powerful.

You are creating an invisible path of energy that is connecting to your intention, making it more "real." When you manifest something so substantial, it's easier to follow down this path. At the very least, from this grid you will get the reassurance and validation that your goals are achievable. It will set that intention in your own mind to be even stronger, so you're razor-focused on achieving what you set out to.

Keep this grid in a meditation spot to help increase the energy you're putting out. You can meditate directly in front of it or you can set it off to the side. The longer you let your grid sit out, the more it will be able to charge. This means it will be able to absorb more powerful energies. If you dismantle your grid and stash the crystals away immediately, it will break the connection these crystals have created with each other. Let that connection grow and increase so it will provide you with the energy you need to fulfill your intention. If you can set it out for a full moon cycle, that will make it even more powerful.

Meditating with this will make it easier to focus on the intention you had written down. When your mind starts to wander during meditation or in a time when you need to be focused, the grid will be there. Follow the path you created with the crystal quartz and study the connections these have to one another. You will find that spending time with the chart alone is enough to add charge to your crystals.

4

MEDITATION WITH CRYSTALS

If you're a seasoned meditator, you know doing so with crystals is very important. Meditation is a mental process, but adding crystals makes it a more physical one. Adding mindfulness to these practices will help you stay on track. If you're a beginning meditator and starting with crystals as well, you are giving yourself a head start that will make it more natural to ease into these thought patterns. Crystals have soothing and healing properties important for anyone looking to recover from a damaged mentality.

Crystals are beautiful for mediation and keep you safe when you carry them with you. Do you ever feel strange when you've forgotten your keys or wallet after leaving home? Meditating without crystals can sometimes feel like this after you've been practicing for a while because they play such a vital role when charging your energy.

You can also wear crystals. They can be worn around your neck and can hang in front of your heart. They can be on display to pick up energy around you, or they can be hidden away and used only for your protection. You can make a crown of crystals to wear when you are meditating. Rings adorned with crystals give you a bit of a power boost, especially with tasks you're performing with your hands.

Most importantly, using them for meditation helps better direct your energies. Crystals aren't just shiny, sparkling objects. They are collections of energy, and taking time out of your day to focus on this enhances their abilities.

Meditation takes you away from the chaos of the day. A crystal serves as an object to remind you of the beauty of the world. When so much stress piles on top of us, it's easy to forget about the greater things in life. A crystal combined with a grounding meditative practice enriches your perspective to truly see all the beauty that surrounds you.

The natural elements that create crystals provide a more grounding element than anything else. Connecting with plants, dirt, water, and other outside sources reminds us that we are alive and we are an important role on this planet. Seeing the magic of these simple aspects in life is enlightening and refreshing.

USING CRYSTALS FOR MEDITATION

Remember your intention when meditating. This will be the focal point you have. It shouldn't be a huge goal that you hope to achieve by the end of meditation. For example, "healing from the emotional trauma of my abusive parents" is a great intention, but it will not be cured in one session. Even just five minutes of meditation could bring you to a life-changing realization, but it's important that you consistently practice for the best results.

Crystals can surround you. If you'd like, for these meditations you can create your own grid, at which you are the center. Surrounding yourself in a circle of crystals is a great way to channel the energy of them all at once. Try doing this for the chakra meditation if you'd like! I have provided specific instructions you can try, but I never want to pressure anyone into a method they are uncomfortable with. You know your intention and you know the crystals you've chosen. Experiment with them but stick to what works for you.

You can simply hold these crystals. Doing so keeps you more connected than anything as your hands are the strongest channels into your mindset. They present the opportunity to give or take. They feel and identify. They mold and shape. They create and destroy. These vessels of life will ground you in your meditation when feeling the full force of nature throughout the process. They can be placed on the specific body part you want to heal. I will talk about this further when setting up for the meditations.

CREATING YOUR MEDITATION SPACE

The space you meditate in will greatly affect your results. You should choose a space that you feel completely comfortable in. It should be quiet, tranquil, and protected. You can't expect to heal in the same space where you are constantly stressed out. If you are limited on space and need to reuse a spot with negative energy, make sure to give it an intense spiritual cleansing with sage and other incense.

You should also focus on finding a unique space. By dedicating one specific spot to meditation, you will make it easier for your mind to fall into a relaxing space when it comes time to do these mental exercises. Dedicating a room, corner, or a spot outside in a yard or park is best. If you are limited, simply choose a spot you do nothing else in, like the foot of your bed or even just the opposite side of a couch you commonly sit on.

Pick one spot where nothing "bad" happens. Good vibrations should pass through this area. Avoid walkways with a ton of traffic. Moving further away from the hotspots of the house like the kitchen or front door will also help you find a more tranquil energy.

Scent is an important part of a space. Scent can trigger our memories or relax us. Try using natural scents like herbs, lavender, and other floral scents. They can help make you feel at peace and as if you are outside.

Noise is also a crucial factor. Small background noises like birds chirping and the wind blowing are fine. If necessary, wear headphones or earplugs to drown out traffic or construction work. During guided meditations, use headphones if you can't hear the recordings.

Now, consider your comfort level. Do you prefer lying down? Will you fall asleep too easily if you do this? Can you sit or stand? Find the level that works for you and experiment with different meditation positions until you discover what you like.

Having a spiritual connection also improves your ability to focus while meditating. This can take many forms. A garden, for example, is filled with life. A beautiful view out of a certain window can be inspiring. If your space has a spiritual connection such as this, it could make it more natural for you to find peace and harmony here.

Find special placement for your crystals. They shouldn't just be kept in a bag in the corner or randomly arranged in a box.

Lay them out and take time to notice them. Study their cracks and crevices and appreciate their natural beauty.

Do not let this space become disturbed. Kids might come in begging for attention, storage might pile up if it goes unused, and other outside sources can break the energy. Do your best to keep this spot as mystically neat and pure as possible. Cleanse it on a deeper level as needed. Of course you might dust and sweep and mop, but spiritual cleansing is also essential. You can do this with the use of sage or an air diffuser with specific essential oils.

COMMON MISTAKES TO AVOID

One of the biggest mistakes beginning crystal users make is expecting that only one meditation session is needed. After one simple sesion of just five minutes you might feel a bit better. But that does not mean you are cured forever. Each meditation session gets easier, and you will gain more from them as you increase your strengths. At the same time, ongoing effort is required if you want to see true growth. Think of it like going to the gym. If you were trying to lose 100 pounds, you wouldn't just go once and then never exercise again. It would take time to see results and you'd have to put in a lot of work before you got to live through the benefits.

Some people believe meditation is about forcing your mind to shut off. Then they get frustrated because the thoughts never stop! This is a mistake because by doing this, we suppress memories. We force out thoughts and then we feel guilty for having any at all. The thoughts will never stop coming in. Meditation isn't about blocking a hole. It's about managing the flow of what comes out of it and knowing that it's perfectly fine and normal to let these thoughts pour out.

When it comes to crystal use, there are mistakes beginners will make involving these as well. Be cautious of how powerful you might believe they are. Sometimes we struggle to see our own abilities. While crystals are magnificently formed, they will not give you the magical force to win the lottery or lose weight overnight.

Some believe crystals will do all the work. Unfortunately this is another false belief. confronting negative thoughts, admitting your weaknesses, and recognizing your strengths can be uncomfortable. However, it is this exact trio of mental progress that is required if we ever want to turn our lives around for the better. Crystals will help make that process easier, but you will still be the one doing the bulk of the work.

Quantity does not always matter when it comes to crystals. You can have 100 crystals surrounding you but if you don't know how to direct that energy, they will all be useless.

Though you might get excited and want to buy a bunch of crystals right away, start small. You can start small with quarter-sized crystals, or you can keep it simple with a tiny budget of only one or two. This way, you can get to know these crystals and really find a deeper connection to give you the chance to grow with these precious gemstones.

Crystals are your own tools. Little is known about how much they actually work in regard to a measurable scale. Some will state they owe their life to crystals while others continue to doubt their validity. Don't create expectations for what you will get from them based on others. You might feel immense power immediately or it could take a bit of time to see substantial results. Regardless of what occurs in this process, be patient and look for growth where you can, no matter how small.

Do not believe you have to fall into a certain idealism to properly use crystals. They are what you want to make of them. We all felt pain in our own unique way, so now it is time to heal that aching in an equally specific fashion.

5

GUIDED MEDITATION WITH CRYSTALS

This first meditation is focused on cleansing and building. It is a starting point to get you more closely connected with your overall goal. This intention should center around healing in some way, but as an individual you should seek a unique outcome that will aid in your healing process.

The stress has been clouding our minds for too long. If you are a beginner meditator, the first thing to know about this process is that it will require a bit of practice. The goal is to let your mind run free and be guided by my words. Giving your focus back to the natural flow of elements enables your brain to truly reset. The clutter of your thoughts can keep you connected to things that only end up setting you back. Allow your mind to flow free as I travel through the next three meditation sessions.

These long-form meditations will be performed to help cleanse and heal from past trauma. Once this secret has been unlocked within you, it will become a natural process you can perform on your own. This deep feeling is only uncovered by a willingness to discover a deeper meaning. Harnessing self-healing powers alleviates pains built from the past while also creating a protecting coat against the future.

The small tears in your soul from different adversities we've experienced have been eating away at our energy. Our thoughts are given to distant memories and old hurt that only takes up space in our body, mind, and soul. Giving away too much of our heart leaves us sad and broken, unable to move forward.

Some things will still attack you even after your emotional healing journey, but at the end of the day you will still be in charge. Instead of a crumbling statue, you are now steel. Instead of a wilting flower, you have a strong stalk like a sunflower.

Visualize something dirty that you recently cleaned. Was it your car? Did you paint an old room? Did you have an especially crusty pan after cooking dinner recently?

Think of your emotions like you do this dirty object. Something happened that caused the buildup, and now it is time to scrub it away. While you might be able to do a physical cleanup in a day, the cleanup of your emotional state can take a bit longer.

Take into this meditation your intention and desired outcome. What are you cleaning? How are you planning to grow? What vision do you have for yourself at the end of this process?

This meditation will help fine-tune that intention so your outcome becomes clearer. At first, you might simply want to heal from the things that have hurt you even before recognizing everything that had caused pain.

Find your way to your perfect meditation spot and totally let your body expand and relax. Let go of the tension inside every part of your body and feel it drip away like water. This meditation is for targeting general anxiety around healing. If you are in a peaceful night-time setting you could drift to sleep after. It could also be used during the day as a way to energize and revitalize you before conquering the rest of the day. Remember to perform it in a safe place and not when driving in case you drift away to sleep. Keep your mind open and allow my words to guide you through the cleansing and healing process. Focus on your breathing and begin the meditation when you are ready.

THE MEDITATION

For this first meditation, I recommend holding the crystal of choice with both hands and placed on your abdomen. If it is more comfortable, you can keep your hands by your side and the crystal next to you. When I reference holding the crystal, simply envision yourself doing so rather than actually looking down. Keep your eyes closed and allow yourself to become fully relaxed.

The crystal is growing in connection to your chest. You and the crystal are sharing energies now. This means with every breath in you take, a vibration leaves the crystal. With every breath you let out, energy is transferred back in.

Together you are growing. You can feel your stomach rise as air comes in. It soothes you to send that breath down into this crystal. You are breathing positive energy into it now. You have a goal in mind. It is not too specific, but that is OK. That is the point of this journey we are set to begin. You can discover your desires further as we immerse ourselves in this healing meditation.

You are at peace now. Keep your eyes gently closed so as to decrease all the tension in your face. Listen for the sound of your breathing. Feel as the air helps your chest to rise and notice how it falls as you release the breaths.

With each breath you take, you let go of more of your surroundings. You are drifting away, and everything is getting dark. This does not scare you. You are simply becoming more engulfed in nothingness. Complete relaxation is taking over now.

Breathe in. Breathe out.

When I count down from five, you will be immersed in total darkness. The thoughts will have left your mind.

Five... Four... Three... Two... One...

As your breathing increases, a white light begins to emerge. It comes in flashes and only expands as you breathe in. With each breath out, you are recharging and preparing to bring more energy in.

The white light begins to engulf you, then suddenly a scene is set right before your eyes. This is a peaceful and serene area. A thick blanket of grass lines a clear rocky trail upward. You cannot see what is ahead but you know that you are in a lush, welcoming place.

As you are climbing the hill, you feel some strain in your legs. It is not much, however. You are simply taking one step up at a time. You don't know what lies ahead, but the gravel being pushed back beneath your feet serves as a reminder of just how much you are able to push forward.

Climbing up this hill is a representation of your healing journey. At first you are going to need to climb over this initial bump. Once you have managed to make it to the point, it will all be easy work as you walk downhill.

The trees represent the growth of nature. Everywhere you look there is life. The bright green leaves reach up as high as possible to the beaming sun above.

Breathe in with your crystal. Let your fingers feel the crevices in this stone. They run over the edges and remind you of the natural elements of the world around us. One... Two... Three... Breathe your energy into the crystal to be cleansed now. Three... Two... One...

Nature coats the trees as ivy grows up around their trunks and moss dots the stones below. More lively forms of life begin emerging as you notice birds perched in trees and mushrooms popping up between the grass. The climb up this hill is still going, but you are enjoying the jaunt. If you had not chosen to take this glorious path, you would not be able to appreciate all of the beauty that surrounds you.

Strong roots stretch into the ground that hold the trees into place. They serve as reminders of just how deep things can go when it doesn't always seem like it from above. The bottomless roots of the trees stretch deeper than you could even fathom and they will always remain there. You can cut the top of the tree off, but you would have to fully dig it up if you wanted to get rid of it once and for all.

But you don't want to get rid of it. You appreciate the way the trees have been able to grow around anything in their way. No matter what the circumstances might be, a tree will always dig its roots deep and climb up towards the sky.

Breathe in with your crystal. Feel as the energy expands as you allow this stone to sink deeper into who you are. One... Two... Three... Breathe your energy into the crystal to be cleansed now. Three... Two... One... It is bouncing with your energy. It is absorbing your positive emotions.

Rocks show us everything that we have lived through. They are a representation of hardened minerals and other materials from the very beginnings of our planet. Rocks are everywhere, but crystals don't always make as bold of an appearance. These rocks wear away into sand and dirt and will continue to transform overtime. They are made up of the sand and dirt. This culmination of materials provides significant value to the ecosystem. Bugs make their way underneath for a home. Deer lick them for a salty treat. Other critters can perch up on them to view the world around. Even the most boring rock provides vibrational energy.

Beauty surrounds you. Some dead branches pop up here and there. You might see a scary snake or a big, nasty spider. But none of this is frightening now. You are safe and you are in the clear.

Breathe in with your crystal as you get closer to the top of where you were initially climbing toward. One... Two... Three... Breathe your energy into the crystal to be cleansed now. Three... Two... One...

As you crest the hill, you notice a cleansing bath. You walk toward it; the water is crystal clear. The gleaming sparkle it gives off is inviting and you step right in. You feel the warmth take over your body, starting all the way at the bottoms of your feet. It is the perfect temperature; not too hot, not too cold. The water engulfs you and provides a natural support system.

There are some fish that swim around you. They don't bother you whatsoever. These groups of fish represent your thoughts. Sometimes they swim a little too close for comfort. You might grow fearful. You might get attached to one and watch its every move. However, each fish eventually passes away. Each one continues to a new destination. Though you hold such an intense fear over them initially, everything becomes just fine in the end and works out in a way exactly as it should. This can be a representation of how you might grow fearful and give into an anxious thought, only for everything to turn out perfectly fine and normal in the end.

You and the crystal are cleansing together and still breathing in and out. You are feeling more connected to it. In this vision, look down at the crystal in your hands. It is growing more intense; you can physically feel the vibrations as they pass through your fingers. The energy spreads to the water around you, which makes it even easier to feel these powers.

You enjoy the pleasantly changing temperatures of the water. It does not affect you in any way. You are becoming one with the water. You are sinking deeper and deeper into it.

Breathe in with your crystal. One... Two... Three... Breathe your energy into the crystal to be cleansed now. Three... Two... One...

You decide to get out of the water now and continue on your journey. There is a break in the trees and in between them you can see an intensely blue sky peeking in. As you take a step forward, you become drier until you can feel the sun fully kiss your skin.

You come along a beach. As you breathe in deeply, the smells of the water and of the nature around you are overwhelming. You can feel your crystal becoming charged by the bright, joyous scene in front of you.

This is your own private beach. There is no one else around. There isn't a single soul who is going to disturb you. You continue to hold your crystal as you walk forward toward a lone beach chair. It's facing the water directly on the shore with the bottom half partially submerged. This is your chair. This is exactly the spot you are supposed to be in.

You watch one by one as birds fly away as you sit down in the chair. In the sky high above you, birds are doing their nightly ritual dancing. It is time for everyone to find their place as the sun begins to set. You peacefully look out over the water and are overwhelmed with beauty. The bright purple, pink, and blue sky creates a gradient unlike anything you have seen before.

Grains of sand blow in the wind. They also serve as a reminder of the vastness of the world. Each grain of sand blows away and another comes along, just like the thoughts that pass through your mind.

Shells wash up on shore and collect in crevices. Some will stay there for eternity, while others wash away with the next wave. The waves cleanse your feet as you continue to sit partially submerged. It feels refreshing and energizing to let this kind of emotion take power over your body. You are in a deeper state of relaxation than you thought possible.

This process reminds you that you are capable of healing. In a world filled with so much beauty, how can we take any other choice? Though you have lived through challenging and traumatic moments, your thoughts will eventually blow away in the wind. You are washed of the person you used to be. You are changed forever because of your trauma and that can be a good thing. Now you know more. You have a deeper understanding of life.

Let these thoughts flood your mind as you continue to look out at the sky.

The air lifts you up and gives you life. It passes energy from other living things. Breathe in and feel the powerful air soothe you.

The vastness of the shore represents possibilities. Despite the journey that it took to get here, here you are now. This is where you are supposed to be. There might have been a bit of an uphill climb, but it was worth it because you wouldn't have been able to see the things you see now.

The past that has built this has been important. This is just one step in your overall growth and development. You are going to come out of this stronger than you thought you were when initially enduring the painful experiences. Your resilience and motivation will not only surprise you, but it will create a positive cycle that will inspire you.

It's what continues to build in the future that will become most valuable. Look at the splendor of the beach. Continue to breathe in as you remember the endless possibilities such a world of beauty has to offer.

Breathe in deeply as you connect to the crystal. One... Two... Three... Breathe out as you let your negative energies dissipate. Breathe in again. Now breathe out. Three... Two... One...

You close your eyes in this vision and become connected back to the real version of yourself. Pass your hands over the crystal you chose for the meditation. This now holds the energy of your future. It will serve as a reminder that no matter how tough times get, you will be able to pull yourself out. Regardless of the struggles you endure, things will pass.

This crystal is filled with your intention. You saw a bright future where you could enjoy nature, connect to something meaningful, and, most importantly, find peace. This crystal is your guide, companion, and unconditional support system.

The crystal has cleansed the negative energy transferred into it. You can additionally cleanse it or set it out in the moon to let it become charged.

Continue this breathing pattern as needed. I'm going to count down from ten. When I reach one, you can either fall

CRYSTAL HEALING MEDITATION

asleep or go on with your day. For a further meditation session, continue with the next long-form one I have provided.

Ten... Nine... Eight... Seven... Six.... Five... Four... Three... Two... One...

6

HEALING MEDITATION WITH CRYSTALS

To truly heal, we must find inner peace. One method to do this is to open your chakras. Your chakras are the parts of your body where your energies are the most concentrated. This energy center is often visualized as a spinning wheel. When there are blockages - like stress or trauma - that can keep these wheels from turning. If one wheel stops spinning, the rest will also suffer, meaning we are not living life to the fullest or reaching our greatest potentials. By increasing awareness of this energy, it becomes easier to harvest and use for good intentions.

These energy planes provide us with better emotional management. If you are out of touch with your chakras and they are clogged, it could lead to emotional distress. Open chakras that are nurtured will allow for better emotional management.

When you are aware of your inner energy, it's all the easier to get energy from outside sources, such as crystals. This meditation will be focused on opening and cleansing your chakras. The point will be to keep you more connected to these planes of energy to elicit greater healing.

Each chakra is located in a very important part of your body. Though you cannot physically see a chakra, it is believed that they are spinning discs of energy in the vital parts of your anatomy (Butler, 2016).

For this meditation, you can pick out crystals specifically for each chakra in order to induce a more open nature. Each chakra has a color associated with it, so it's helpful to have a crystal attached to this specific color, which I'll go over now.

The colors follow along in a rainbow pattern. A rainbow only appears when the right pattern of light is formed. By opening your chakras, you allow this pattern of light to flow through you as they connect to one another. This enlightening will lead to more clarity and understanding as you grow closer to your mentality.

The first is your root chakra, which is associated with red. This spinning wheel of energy is red because it is driven by passion. Your root chakra is the foundation for the rest and is associated with the bottom of your spine. Think of it as the grounding aspect that keeps you in place.

Next, orange represents your sacral chakra. This circle is in your groin area and lower than the belly button. It is connected to sexual intuition, pleasure, and abundance.

Yellow is the color of the solar plexus chakra, which is in your stomach. It's connected to confidence and self-worth, which is important for intuition.

The heart chakra is attached to green. This is the center of all the chakras and is located where you would expect: your chest. It involves happiness, peace, and love.

Blue represents the throat chakra. This represents your voice and is found in the throat. It represents how you express yourself and the connection you have to the truth.

Indigo is the third eye chakra. This forehead circle is connected to your ability to see and understand.

Finally, the last color is violet, though it is sometimes also represented as white. This represents your crown chakra. This is the hardest chakra to fully connect to and represents your overall spiritual connection.

This chakra meditation is a perfect one to charge your crystal grid, especially if you have chosen rainbow colors to represent each of your chakras. Remember to connect them all using a clear quartz. Write down your intentions so that with each chakra cleanse you are connected back to this deeper purpose.

If you don't want to use your crystal grid, you could also place a specific colored stone on each of your chakras. If you'd like to just use one crystal of your choice, you could place this on your forehead where your third eye chakra is, or you could place it on your stomach for comfort.

As with all meditation, practice this in a comfortable space. Laying down is fine, especially if you're choosing to place the crystals directly on your body. For an advanced method, try this one sitting upright. You can place the bottom of your feet together pointed at your crystal grid in front of you. Some find more efficiency when keeping their eyes open during a chakra meditation. As we travel through each chakra, you can focus your energy on the corresponding crystal as a method for easier opening.

This meditation can be repeated as needed, so experiment to find what feels comfortable. When you are ready, you can begin the next meditation.

THE MEDITATION

The word "chakra" is translated from the Sansrkit word for "wheel."

Let the crystal's color turn from scary to positive. See it in a healthy light.

Every chakra has its own vibrations. Remember to connect with your crystals throughout these meditations.

Breathe in for one, two, three, four, and five. Breathe out for five, four, three, two, and one. Let the colors of the crystals wash over you.

Breathe in the color and breathe it out. One, two, three, four, and five, then five, four, three, two, and one.

Start at the very bottom of your body, where your root chakra exists. At the bottom of your spine is a spinning disk of energy that keeps you grounded to reality. This chakra burns red and that is the color it is often associated with. Envision a red glow coming from the bottom of your tailbone now.

Red in general provides an alertness.

The root is where your body's intuition lies.

This root chakra is the basis for how you protect yourself.

Fear can block your root chakra.

Lacking courage in yourself will certainly cause a blockage at the root chakra.

Self-doubt will prevent you from gaining the things you know you fully deserve.

This red energy can become alert if we are not careful. It might cause you to lash out on others.

Stomach problems and aching pains in the lowest of your belly could indicate a greater issue with the root chakra. It can affect your bladder or cause bowel issues.

Focus on soothing this chakra now. Breathe in a glowing red, then breathe out and let it disperse through the air. Envision the red crystal you have or imagine that a clear quartz you are using is glowing red now as you charge it.

Soothe this burning red.

Let the anger dissipate.

You are not frustrated.

The peace is growing inside of you.

Think of this red as bright energy.

A juicy cherry pops into your mind.

A red velvet couch wraps you up in warmth.

The darkest part of a sunset right before it goes down for the day.

Envision yourself inside the red crystal. Whether you are using a quartz or a specific red crystal for the root chakra, keep your eyes closed and focus on what it would look like if you were inside of it.

You start to grow, and as you do the crystal becomes smaller and smaller

This red is the closest burning point to the flame that ignites your spirit.

Breathe in for one, two, three, four, and five. Breathe out for five, four, three, two, and one. Let these colors wash over you.

Breathe in the color and breathe it out. One, two, three, four, and five. Five, four, three, two, and one.

Move slowly up as you become aware of the sacral chakra. This energy can be felt within your pelvic area. Below your belly button exists a bursting orange ball of energy. It is connected to the root chakra by this same passion and energy, orange like a bright sunset or a crisp, sweet orange.

Your sacral chakra can be clogged by a lack of passion and creativity. This vibrant energy is needed for you to reach your greatest dreams. Feeling stunted in progression might have created a barrier that prevented substantial change. Suffering in one's love life might have killed your passion.

Sometimes we are led too deeply by lust while ignoring meaningful passion. Chasing instant pleasure serves as a distraction from the longer-term but more rewarding challenges in life. A lack of emotional management can lead to suffering beyond just ourselves.

You are going to heal from this now.

Feel as the blockages in your sacral chakra are now opening.

This point of energy must be cleansed to be free from the trauma that existed in the past. Allow this peaceful energy to fill you now.

Take back your creativity and remember that it is your own. It is something you express to enhance your understanding and display your perspective.

You are a sacred being.

Let orange wash over you like the sunset that emerges every day. This represents a brand-new beginning; an opportunity to be yourself. Breathe in the fresh, beaming glow as you feel your stomach rise. Breathe out the hot stickiness that has kept you trapped. You are not a fly stuck in glue. You are a free bird chasing the sun.

Think of a deep orange that's a blend of bronze and gold, engulfing you in reassurance and comfort. This vibrancy is unique and sets you apart from the rest. Picture a juicy and dripping mango. This sweetness represents the delectable taste you will get from life.

Imagine a friendly and curious goldfish. Picture the orange that keeps you safe. Let this power you now. Your chakra is becoming clearer and clearer. You are allowing a free-flowing path to exist between the two chakras. Your root is connecting stronger to your sacral chakra. This helps to drive intuition and reassure you that you are powerful.

Think of a delicious dreamsicle on a hot summer day. This cool summer treat alleviates your stress and brings about a childlike nature. The sweet juices of the melting popsicle blend perfectly with the refreshing ice cream underneath. It reminds you of summer vacations, beaches, and happy times.

Orange is the flicker of a candle on a cold and blue winter day. It is the light from a window that lets us know someone is home and we are not alone.

Orange is the color of the vibrant fall leaves. It represents a changing period in when things are coming to an end.

It's the horizon of the night as the sun lowers before a new day.

Allow yourself to be stimulated. Breathe in this powerful orange and breathe out the negativity. Let this chakra wash over you like a relaxing bath. It stimulates the perfect blend between the red root chakra and the bouncing orange sacral one.

You are vibrant with energy. This powers motivation, excitement, and thrill.

The blockages in your chakra energy system are unclogging.

You are your own best friend and it serves as a reassuring reminder that everything will turn out perfectly fine.

Breathe in for one, two, three, four, and five. Breathe out for five, four, three, two, and one. Let these colors wash over you.

Breathe in the color and breathe it out. One, two, three, four, and five. Five, four, three, two, and one.

The next chakra is your solar plexus. Feel this chakra deep in your stomach, where you get that familiar "butterflies" sensation. Allow this area to become soothed and peaceful now. You are transforming buried intuition into a driving force leading you exactly where you should be going.

This chakra is hidden in the stomach close to the core of the body. The friendly yellow color is the true gold; your intuition.

This is a neutral and welcoming color that's inviting to any and all parties. It is a friendly reminder of comfort and support, which can be greatly needed in challenging times of constant change.

The things that block it are now becoming part of the past as you allow this chakra to open. Imagine you have a bright yellow crystal that is bouncing around. If you have one in front of you, picture a glow coming from the yellow intensity now.

Yellow is bold. If we don't see it this way, it becomes akin to a precursor to an alarm, like a yellow stoplight or caution sign. Appreciate the boldness of yellow. Breathe in as you let this warm color fill you with familiarity.

Self-esteem issues related to our abilities are controlled within this specific chakra. Let go of all the thoughts that trapped you in negativity. Take this moment to remind yourself of your worth. Take time to nurture the way that you see yourself.

You are strong.

You are brave.

You are growing.

You are safe.

You are your own protector.

This is the topmost of the three bottom chakras. It can become blocked by a general weakness you have in yourself. But you have now opened the door. Breathe in vibrant, exciting yellow. Breathe out muted and sick yellow. You are not infected. You are filled to the brim with joy and happiness.

This is blocked when we are so afraid of ourselves that it begins to spread to other people. Others do not doubt you. They believe in your abilities and trust in your talents.

Remember that you are confident. Breathe in reassuring yellow and breathe out the stale idea that you are not good enough.

You are confident.

You are responsible.

You have a sense of purpose.

You are motivated by a legitimate passion.

You do not depend on others.

You are aware of your own worth.

Let these thoughts fill you. Remember your own worth. This driving force in your gut will keep propelling you to new and exciting opportunities. Breathe in as you charge your crystal with a bright yellow energy. Picture yourself back inside the crystal. It is now glowing and changing smoothly from red to orange to yellow. The relation of these colors is so seamless that it simply demands our focus as we continue to meditate.

Let your mind wander up to the next chakra. This perfect transition from yellow to green offers you more peace and comfort within yourself.

Breathe in for one, two, three, four, and five. Breathe out for five, four, three, two, and one. Let these colors wash over you.

Breathe in the color and breathe it out. One, two, three, four, and five. Five, four, three, two, and one.

Open up your Heart Chakra.

This deep chest spinning plate of energy is what keeps your world moving. There are no emotions felt physically in the heart, but they will manifest in this plane. A hateful spirit, harsh judgement, and interpersonal anger will block the green flow that comes from your heart chakra.

We can get stuck on old relationships, or at least the feelings we connect to them. It's easy to replay old things over and over while building up ideas of things that do not exist. It can be hard to trust.

Your heart wants to heal now. It is begging for you to put the time and effort in to elicit true and meaningful change.

You feel your heart growing now as you focus on opening up to new possibilities. You are aware of the strengths and weaknesses you've been exhibiting, especially in regard to other people.

Allow your heart to become more open. Breathe in as you feel your chest expand. You are connecting to the natural green that flows out from your chest, where your heart chakra is located. You are not opening it weakly. You are letting others into this heart again.

Breathe in green. Feel your chest rise. Breathe out old, sick green. Let go of negativity.

Breathe in. Breathe out.

You are at the halfway point of your chakras now. They are all connecting better than ever. The colors are seamlessly blending, working in a rainbow pool that spreads throughout your body. This positive energy is normal, earned, and should be fully appreciated when granted on a different spiritual plane.

Our hearts don't have to burn red and passionate but instead give off a green color. This alleviates tension. Think of a blossoming green canopy. Think of the thick stalks that hold up flowers. Green is the grass beneath our feet. Breathe in the natural feelings of this earthly staple.

The chakra heart is green because we are connected to everything. Breathe in green. Breathe out negativity.

We are the earth that surrounds us. We eat green. We are powered by green. We let this color remain vibrant in our minds. Connect to your crystals now. They are green. They are found in the earth. They were carefully crafted by the same beautiful masterminds that brought you trees and grass. The secrets and recipes of Mother Earth may never be uncovered, but for now you find peace in this beauty.

We are the plants that we see.

Don't be afraid of your own emotions. Commit to yourself. Let go now.

You feel your heart opening. Your love is expanding. Your curiosity is turning more vibrant.

Recognize your own needs and wants. They are becoming more precise than ever before. When you are healing, you are discovering yourself. You are getting rid of the hurt that others have caused in the past. You are not the words that others have stated. You are above the labels you have been given.

Breathe in. Breathe out. Breathe in. Breathe out.

Love unconditionally. You are becoming more awakened. You are realizing the strength that exists in your heart. Love and emotions are not a weakness. They are our strengths.

Feel the relaxation drip through every part of your body.

Think of green as abundance—but not as the color of paper bills. There is abundance in nature around us. We are surrounded by beauty.

Breathe in for one, two, three, four, and five. Breathe out for five, four, three, two, and one. Let these colors wash over you. You are over halfway through now.

Breathe in the color and breathe it out. One, two, three, four, and five. Five, four, three, two, and one.

Your throat chakra radiates blue through the rest of your body. This calming color soothes you and serves as a reminder of the familiarity of communication.

Blue represents empathy and the one thing that connects us all—water. This universal color is found everywhere. It represents communication, as that is how we connect. Blue is the color of the messages we send, and social media apps used to participate in that level of communication, like Facebook, Twitter, Tumblr, and Linkedin.

Not living true to yourself will take this blue away. Breathe in deeper than you have throughout this entire meditation.

You are replenishing your ability to speak your mind. These thoughts are becoming natural. They are filling you with confidence and the reminder that you are good enough.

Not properly expressing your needs and choosing to keep important things from others only keep this chakra blocked. Allow the passage of energy to continue to flow upwards by opening this important part of your energy field.

Realize your voice is worth something. Even the smallest sparkle on your favorite crystal provides an intense amount of beauty.

You are aware of your emotions and expressions. They flow naturally out of you like water. You are more relaxed than ever. You are at peace with this natural flow of energy. It occurs to you to fuel more important areas around it much like a waterfall would.

Connect to the deeper voice in the back of your mind. You know what it is saying to you. There are words hidden there and you know how to unlock them. This fills you with a soothing blue. Breathe in as you envision the crystal all around you. This is an absorption of the sky. It is a collection of water shades.

Breathe in for one, two, three, four, and five. Breathe out for five, four, three, two, and one. Let these colors wash over you.

Breathe in the color and breathe it out. One, two, three, four, and five. Five, four, three, two, and one.

Moving up to your forehead, you will feel the third eye. Unlocking all the rest thus far though this peaceful meditation has made it feel natural for a surge of energy to go straight to your third eye. This indigo color can be represented in your clear quartz crystal or one that matches the deep purple and blue hues that casts a unique haze throughout your body.

Indigo is the color of the night sky when we are able to have a greater understanding of our surroundings. As your mind settles for the day, important thoughts will travel in and out of your brain.

It's when you're in bed with the moonlight shining that you are able to bring deeper memories to your mind. Dreams reveal hidden secrets as the stars kiss us from up high. This deep indigo wraps us up in a creative yet familiar environment. Dreams flow in and out naturally. Do not try to force them away. As your third eye continues to open more and more, you will begin to connect back to some of your dreams.

Your third eye can get blocked by almost everything you do if you are not careful.

When the third eye is blocked or never even opened in the first place, it can mean missing important things around us. Overlooking important aspects of your life can clutter the third eye.

Fear, jealousy, rage, and other deep, negative emotions will put filters on this third eye's view.

Breathe in a refreshing indigo that adds immense power to your day. Breathe out sticky blue or purple that isn't adding anything to your mentality.

See the hidden signs and connections. They are there. They are reassuring you and filling you with peace.

There are things around you that are leading you in a certain direction. Trust this instinct. The third eye is there for a reason.

Connect back to the crystal. The energy is flowing in and out of it more than ever before. If you are working with a grid, you can feel as though the energy between the crystals is starting to truly heat up.

Suspend your mind momentarily. Don't force things in or out. Simply let them flow in like the deep indigo sky as the sun goes into hiding for the day.

Let natural thoughts flood your brain. Your third eye knows how to filter out the very valuable information that can lead to greater discoveries.

Avoid resistance. Breathe in acceptance. Breathe out resistance.

Investigate and explore. Let the crystal guide you. You have this power. You can feel your third eye buzzing in your forehead. It is exchanging crucial power between your thoughts and your crystals. You are running through the rainbow, seeing the connections. Now we are almost at the end. You are reaching a new spiritual awakening you didn't think was possible. Your crystals are intensely charged, making them even more effective for the next meditation practice you try.

Breathe in for one, two, three, four, and five. Breathe out for five, four, three, two, and one. Let these colors wash over you. Breathe in the color and breathe it out. One, two, three, four, and five. Five, four, three, two, and one.

The last chakra is your crown chakra. This exists as a white glow that surrounds your head in a circular formation. White is the absence—and neutralizer—of all other colors. It manages to be a simple and pure color while adding its own elements of beauty. Think of the peaceful white snow that engulfs a city or the soft white of a cat's belly.

White is beyond color and exists as a blank, clean slate. White is the immaculate spiritual light shining down on you. You feel this radiant vibrancy surrounding your brain. Now that you have unclogged all of the chakras and given them a chance to be cleansed, you will be able to connect them all.

Let the rainbow flow naturally.

The inability to unlock these other chakras will keep your crown from truly shining. Understanding, recognizing, and opening these important areas of your mind will increase your ability to find harmony.

Be mindful of the power that the connection of these chakras creates. Opening these areas doesn't mean you are instantly cured, although it will allow for greater healing.

You are a stabilizer. You are the master of your emotions. Breathe in healthy and positive energy. Breathe out the idea of feeling "stuck."

Find the beauty in life. Breathe in as it serves as a reminder of why you are healing. Let go of the fear of the past. Remember that the future is still yours. Breathe in as you feel peace from this reminder. Breathe out as you let go of the false "comfort" that traumatic discomfort once provided.

Become excited about the future. There is no going back. You know what lies ahead and it will be big and bright.

Find strength in your own abilities. This is your healing journey. It is allowing you to find more and more relaxation.

Let yourself flourish. You are more connected than ever. You are realizing the power of your chakras and these crystals.

They have been identified, cleansed, and you have found awareness in them. Continue to open these chakras and ensure they have not become blocked again.

Take a minute to let each chakra light up with the specific color that has been assigned.

One is for the bright red root chakra. This juicy cherry of spinning energy gives you the reassurance you are in charge. Breathe in red for one, two, three. Breathe energy into your crystals for three, two, and one.

Two is for the friendly orange sacral chakra. The sunset that kisses you goodnight is now transitioning into the next color.

Yellow lightning electrifies your creativity and gives you a deeper intuition. You can feel your willpower growing strong in your stomach. Breathe in red, orange, and yellow. Breathe them out and envision their colors swarming your crystals.

In the middle is your heart, connecting everything else. This green, abundant passion allows you to find a deeper connection to the earth. Breathe in as you realize your abilities to find love, joy, and happiness.

The fifth part of your chakra is a relaxing blue. Your throat chakra is now open, allowing an important, free-flowing relationship to have more beneficial conversations.

Your third-eye chakra is big, open, and ready to explore. You are more aware than you ever have been before, and there is certainly no going back.

Lastly, your white, bright, crown chakra illuminates the rest of your rainbow. You have unlocked these important energy settings. This rejuvenating meditation can be performed as needed. It can also be used to drift away. If you choose to do that right now, please proceed to that. If not, carry on for the remainder of the day.

I am going to count down from twenty-one. Breathe in for three and out for three. As you do this, remember to travel up and down your chakras and through the colors for the greatest spiritual connection.

Twenty-one. Twenty. Nineteen. Eighteen. Seventeen. Sixteen. Fifteen. Fourteen. Thirteen. Twelve. Eleven. Ten. Nine. Eight. Seven. Six. Five. Four. Three. Two. One…

7

RELAXING MEDITATION WITH CRYSTALS

One of the most important parts of healing is setting yourself up for the future. The things that have already happened to us are what keep us fearful and anxious throughout the day. Though these past memories are gone and done, they still haunt us every step of the way.

To heal means to know that the future is going to be all right. No matter what might happen, you will be strong enough to live through life's greatest challenges. If you can foster this belief within yourself, then nothing will be as painful as it was in the past, even if you were to live through it again.

This meditation is one centered on finding peace with who you are and the future that awaits. Life might not have turned out the way we thought it would but that doesn't mean it didn't work out the way that it was intended to. *We are here now* for a reason, and we have lived through what we have for a purpose as well. Throughout this meditation, I will provide you with the peace and serenity that is needed to fight through the things that scare you the most.

The crystals will be used to help connect you to your body. The best way to feel the power from crystals is to immerse yourself in the vibrations they give off. As your intuition increases, so will your abilities to realize that everything that has happened did so for a reason, and everything that will happen in the future is also of some value. This comfortability allows our bodies to feel more relaxed. If you believe you are meant to be in this space at this time, things feel a bit easier to manage.

Trusting yourself will also provide a sense of security. If you are constantly uncomfortable with who you are, it can be very challenging to have faith in your own abilities. You will second-guess your abilities to make the right decision. A choice might be so hard to make that you decide to not make one at all, resulting in a missed opportunity.

To perform these meditations, pick the crystal that is most important to you. Find one that has great intention and a positive energy. Use this to connect you to a deeper meaning. Let these crystals become a physical manifestation of your powers.

Place this crystal on the part of you that needs the most healing. Finding this connecting spot will make the healing more effective. The crystal can act as a sponge to absorb negative vibrations. You can then clean the crystal to replenish the energy. A good crystal to absorb energy is citrine. This crystal is self-cleaning, so you can use it multiple times without having to bathe it yourself.

Place the crystal on your head if you want to clear your thoughts. Fluorite is a great crystal to use for focus and clarity. If in your healing process you find it hard to stay on track and you often lose sight of your goals, a mental reset can help. Opal is also great for establishing better brain health.

Place the crystal on your heart to open your spirit and increase compassion. Rose quartz will be the best for any love-related healing. This is done through healing from the emotional past of your romantic life. It's also an important aspect for learning to love yourself.

Pick your stomach if you are looking to amp up your willpower and intuition. Labradorite is a great crystal for this purpose, as it helps increase your psychic abilities. Amethyst can also be used for this as it's a very cleansing and opening crystal that can make it easier for you to trust your gut.

Put the crystal above your head if you are still seeking more guidance and clarity. Howlite is a good crystal for this as it helps to lead you in the direction you should be going. It's drenched in destiny so it can be good for opening your crown chakra and serving as a guide.

Place the crystal at the bottom of your feet as you are laying down if you are ready to leave the past behind and want a clean slate. Aqua aura can give you a fresh, clean start as you push forward.

You know your intention and what you need the most from this meditation, so find a place most suitable for your crystal. Where you place the crystal should not be causing any pain or discomfort. If it is, pick a new spot. You will be relaxing and finding peace throughout this meditation, so it's crucial that you are as comfortable as possible. For this reason as well, ensure you do this at home in a safe space. Do not listen to this if you are driving a car or even riding on public transportation if you do not know how your body will react. Though these commutes are tempting times to relax, it's even more important that you are in a safe and peaceful place to make the most of the meditation.

This is a great meditation for anyone who will be transitioning into a state of deep sleep, whether it's a refreshing nap or for bed.

For the final meditation, place yourself and your crystals in a comfortable place and begin when you are ready.

THE MEDITATION

Keep your eyes closed and your crystals near. Have them wherever you believe they are going to serve you the most.

Sink as deep as you possibly can into the surface on which you are lying. You will continue to reach a deeper and more comfortable state as I travel throughout this meditation.

Start by deeply controlling your breathing. Breathe in through just your nose right now. In one…two…three…. Out three…two…one….

Breathe in and out now through just your mouth. Breathe in for one… two… three…. Breathe out at this moment for three… two… one….

Now it is time to really regulate. Breathe in through your nose for one… two… three… four… five… Transition gently and now breathe out through your mouth for five… four… three… two… one…

Continue alternating through these patterns of breathing throughout the remainder of the meditation. It is time to move closer toward a more intense and deeper state now. We are going to travel through your entire body to relax every single part. Once you become totally at peace with your physical anatomy, you should have no trouble regulating your thoughts.

Breathe in through your nose for one… two… three… four… five… Breathe out through your mouth for five… four… three… two… one…

Start by noticing the top of your head. You don't have to do anything like touch it or flex it. Simply become aware of its existence. This is the part where everything is hidden. Your mind holds the wonders of your life, your thoughts, your beliefs, and your values. You sleep, you think, you decide, you love, you watch, you listen, and you feel with your brain. As you are tapping into this important part of your mind, your crown chakra begins to buzz. It adds a light feeling that provides an almost euphoric tingle. Becoming aware of the vastness of your mind will ground you in the moment. You felt pain with the same brain that you will be able to heal with. Let your mind become more wondrous now. Feel the deeper connection growing as you allow yourself to accept what has happened and move on from the past.

Notice your ears. This is where you might have taken some verbal damage. Past traumas related to what we have heard do not rob our ears of their abilities. Think of the laughter you've heard. Nothing sounds better than the giggle of an excited baby. What about the laughter of strangers at a restaurant across the room? You might never know what they all thought was funny, but you are reminded that they are enjoying themselves. Think of the laughter of your friends. Your favorite song still rings throughout your eardrums. You can hear your name, the sizzle of your favorite dish cooking, and the relaxing sounds of the ocean. Your ears begin to heal as you become aware of them. You are connecting to your body on a deeper level than ever before.

Breathe in. Breathe out.

Notice your forehead. This is a point of expression. You show others when you are shocked. You share concern, excitement, and confusion with this forehead. It is also where your third eye chakra exists. Picture it now as it sits beneath the surface. You can see things you did not see before, now that you have allowed yourself to enter the healing process.

Breathe in one...two....three. Breathe out three... two... one.

Notice your eyes. They see so many wondrous things. They provide you with a vision of things you adore. You get to study the characteristics of the person you love more than anything. You can see good news and read things that make you feel happy. You can watch your favorite movie and your mouth starts to water at the site of your favorite dish. These eyes have seen hurt. They have seen pain and they understand the anguish that exists in others' eyes as well. Your eyes are healing. They are growing. You would not be able to appreciate the beauty that you do now had you not first seen some harder things initially.

Breathe in. Breathe out.

Notice your nose. You can smell with your nose. It's what opens you up to be able to fully experience delicious food. Your nose touches someone else when you kiss them. You can smell nostalgic scents and enchanting candles that make you feel at home.

Breathe in One...two...three. Breathe out three...two...one.

Notice your cheeks. Your cheeks are the two points on your face that support your smile. How many times have they been sore from laughter? How frequently have you found yourself rubbing your cheeks from smiling all day long? Sometimes that smile has been taken from you. That does not mean you can't get it back. You are the only person in charge of whether you choose to smile today.

Breathe in. Breathe out.

Notice your jaw. So much tension can get stuck in your jaw, but this is where you must release that aching pain now. Your jaw helps you express your feelings. You can communicate by moving your mouth. You share ideas. Your jaw might have been hurt in the past but now it is time to rest and replenish.

Notice the back of your head. This is what some people see so often.

Notice your neck. This is the main trunk of your body. It connects the most important part of your body, your brain, to every other area. Your neck can be so sore and tense. You are letting all of the tension go now. The crystal or crystals you are using are absorbing this pain. You are becoming free from all of that stiffness you've held for so long.

Breathe in one...two...three. Breathe out three...two...one.

Notice your shoulders. These can feel as though they are carrying the world. You will have immense pressure weighing down and sometimes it might be so heavy you feel like you're going to fall over. The crystal is absorbing those burdens. You are able to free yourself from the strains of life as you pass them along to the vibration of the crystals.

Breathe in. Breathe out.

Notice your arms. Your arms carry the world. They hug the people you love. They give to others. They add to your expression. Your arms might have been used to defend you against hurt. You are safe now. You are free from this pain. You are growing and you are healing.

Breathe in. Breathe out.

Notice your hands. Your hands have just as much power as your arms. You can hold someone else's hand. You can touch someone and change them for life. You can create, you can destroy, and you can decide the fate of the things around you. You are going to use your hands for healing moving forward. They will aid in your ability to find strength and alleviation from life's most challenging moments.

Breathe in one...two...three. Breathe out three...two...one.

Notice your chest. Beneath the rise and fall of every breath is a valuable heart that leads you. Your lungs power you through and if you have breasts they might have supported life or will at some point in the future. You are powerful. In such a small space on your body you hold so much strength. Feel a connection from your crystal to this area of your body.

Breathe in. Breathe out.

Notice your abdomen. Tension can build in the pit of your stomach. Things feel overwhelming and you might exacerbate digestive issues. Your stomach is healing now. It realizes that everything is going to be OK.

Breathe in one…two…three. Breathe out three…two…one.

Notice your pelvis. This is another important area. Not only can it contribute to your reproduction, but it also holds a pleasure center of your body. You are healing as you grow stronger toward your masculinity, your femininity, and a place between the two. You are strengthened by your identity in some ways and this can be a very empowering aspect if you want it to be. Knowing who you are is a powerful tool, and only you can define that identity.

Breathe in. Breathe out.

Notice your legs. Your legs have carried you almost everywhere. You can climb stairs and mountains. You can wrap them around someone you love. You can dance. You can run. You can jump. Your legs are powerful. You are confident in your abilities. Your legs hold your knees which connect to your feet and your toes. These are powerful points of your body.

Breathe in one…two…three. Breathe out three…two…one.

You are healing. You are growing. You are becoming the best version of yourself.

Travel up and down your body and pass through the various colors of the rainbow. You will continue to be an astonishing creature that exists in a magnificent way. You keep healing more and more; each day is a new chance to grow.

Everything is going to be perfectly fine. It has all worked out in a way exactly as it should have.

Breathe in through your nose for one... two... three... four... five. Breathe out through your mouth for five... four... three... two... one.

You have been wrung out from stress. You are healing from the deepest traumas, those that have shaken you to your core. You are allowing your body to truly flourish and heal. You are opening yourself up. You are becoming brand new.

Let your body become more and more relaxed. Now you can drift off to sleep as peacefully as possible and entirely comfortable with your body. I am going to count down from ten. Breathe in and out at a comfortable pace. This is the final meditation. You can now drift off to sleep or continue with your day.

Ten... Nine... Eight... Seven... Six... Five... Four... Three... Two... One.

CONCLUSION

The history of healing crystals reveals that they work for people. Even though they aren't a prescription given to ill patients or a method tested frequently, they still have powerful abilities that many people connect to. You can use crystals for your own intended purposes, but remember the power that exists in research as well.

Studying how crystals form can also make your selection process a bit more personalized. What do the methods by which they form reveal about their value? How is this process similar or relatable to something you are going through yourself?

Crystals have many uses, but one of the most effective is their healing abilities. They act as a grounding place where you can find peace and structure. They are manifestations of

CONCLUSION

your own problems or energy use and can take you closer to your goals.

Crystals can have many beneficial effects. They can awaken your spirit. They will make meditation feel like a more normal process. You can find a deep connection to the earth through these natural formations. They have very little side effects and will stay with you for a long time.

Your healing journey is just beginning, so moving forward after this will be an ongoing process. Healing is not something you can rush through; you wouldn't try to walk on a broken ankle before you get an approval from your doctor, would you?

The more time you dedicate to your meditation regimen, the more effective results you will likely see back. Remember to practice with different methods and diversify your abilities to connect on a more spiritual level.

Slowly introduce crystals to the group and take note of how they make you feel. For example, a rose quartz might be often associated with romance, but if you get a motivational vibration from one, who is to say this is false? You will have your own connection to the vibrational energy each crystal gives off, and you, in turn, can choose how that is used.

Heal from the emotional pain. It's OK to let go of the hurt from the past. Recovering from trauma isn't easy, and many

CONCLUSION

will go their entire lives without even trying. However, you hold the key to unlocking a better and brighter future, so now is the time to take the plunge.

Check out more meditations on similar topics to bring you even closer to your spirituality. You can never put too much emphasis on improving your mental health. Repeat these meditations as needed and try different crystals to see how they might change a session. Stay dedicated to yourself and soon enough you will see the full potential of the beautiful person you are becoming.

REFERENCES

Askinosie, H. (2016). Crystals for Intuition & Trusting Your Gut Instincts. https://www.energymuse.com/blog/crystals-for-intuition

Broad, W. (1995). The Core of the Earth May Be a Gigantic Crystal Made of Iron. https://www.nytimes.com/1995/04/04/science/the-core-of-the-earth-may-be-a-gigantic-crystal-made-of-iron.html#:~:text=Deeper%20still%2C%20-pressures%20and%20densities,per-cent%20of%20the%20earth's%20volume.

Butler, N. (2016). A Beginner's Guide to the 7 Chakras and Their Meanings. https://www.healthline.com/health/fitness-exercise/7-chakras

REFERENCES

Crystal Age. (n.d.). A Brief History of Crystals and Healing. https://www.crystalage.com/crystal_information/crystal_history/

Crystal Vaults. (n.d.). Agate Meanings and Uses. https://www.crystalvaults.com/crystal-encyclopedia/agate

Elle. (2020). Healing Crystals - What Are They And How Should You Use Them. https://www.elle.com/uk/life-and-culture/culture/articles/a31572/what-are-healing-crystals-how-to-use-them/

Hurst, K. (n.d.). A Guide To Healing Crystals: 10 Most Effective Healing Stones. https://www.thelawofattraction.com/healing-crystal-guide/

Marshall, L. (2018). Can Crystals Heal? Separating Facets from Facts. https://www.webmd.com/balance/news/20180116/can-crystals-heal-separating-facets-from-facts

Medlicott, C. (2019). 10 Crystals That Cleanse Your Aura. https://www.mysticalone.com/blog/10-crystals-that-cleanse-your-aura/

Monq. (2019). How Many Different Types of Crystals Are There in the World? https://monq.com/eo/crystals-healing-stones/different-types-of-crystals/

Palmer, C. (2020). Crystals for Beginners: The Complete Guide to Understand and Practice the Healing Power of Crystals. Amazon.

Rekstis, E. (2019). Healing Crystals 101. https://www.healthline.com/health/mental-health/guide-to-healing-crystals#1

Satin Crystals. (n.d.). Crown Chakra Crystal Healing. https://satincrystals.com/pages/healing-the-7th-crown-chakra

Shashkevich, A. (2018). Stanford scholar tackles the history of people's obsession with crystals. https://news.stanford.edu/2018/08/09/understanding-peoples-obsession-crystals/

Shurkin J. (2014). News feature: Animals that self-medicate. Proceedings of the National Academy of Sciences of the United States of America, 111(49), 17339–17341. https://doi.org/10.1073/pnas.1419966111

www.ingramcontent.com/pod-product-compliance
Lightning Source LLC
Chambersburg PA
CBHW071905070526
44583CB00016B/1850